CIRCUS
Coloring book for kids

This Coloring book
Belongs to:

....

....

Try Your Coloring Pencil Before Coloring

Try Your Coloring Pencil Before Coloring

Try Your Coloring Pencil Before Coloring

Try Your Coloring Pencil Before Coloring

Try Your Coloring Pencil Before Coloring

Try Your Coloring Pencil Before Coloring

Try Your Coloring Pencil Before Coloring

Try Your Coloring Pencil Before Coloring

Try Your Coloring Pencil Before Coloring

Try Your Coloring Pencil Before Coloring

Try Your Coloring Pencil Before Coloring

Try Your Coloring Pencil Before Coloring

Try Your Coloring Pencil Before Coloring

Try Your Coloring Pencil Before Coloring

Try Your Coloring Pencil Before Coloring

Try Your Coloring Pencil Before Coloring

Try Your Coloring Pencil Before Coloring

Try Your Coloring Pencil
Before Coloring

Try Your Coloring Pencil

Before Coloring

Try Your Coloring Pencil Before Coloring

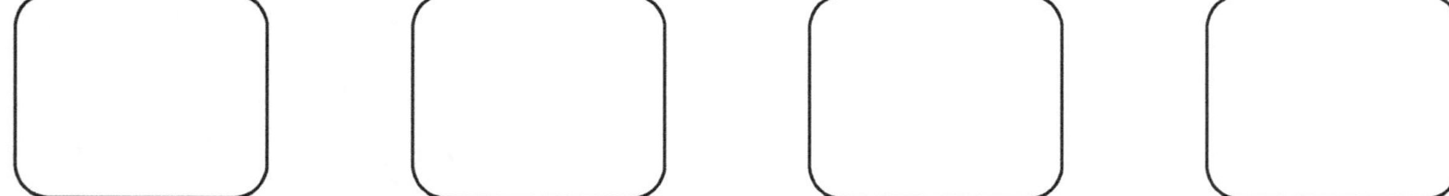

Try Your Coloring Pencil Before Coloring

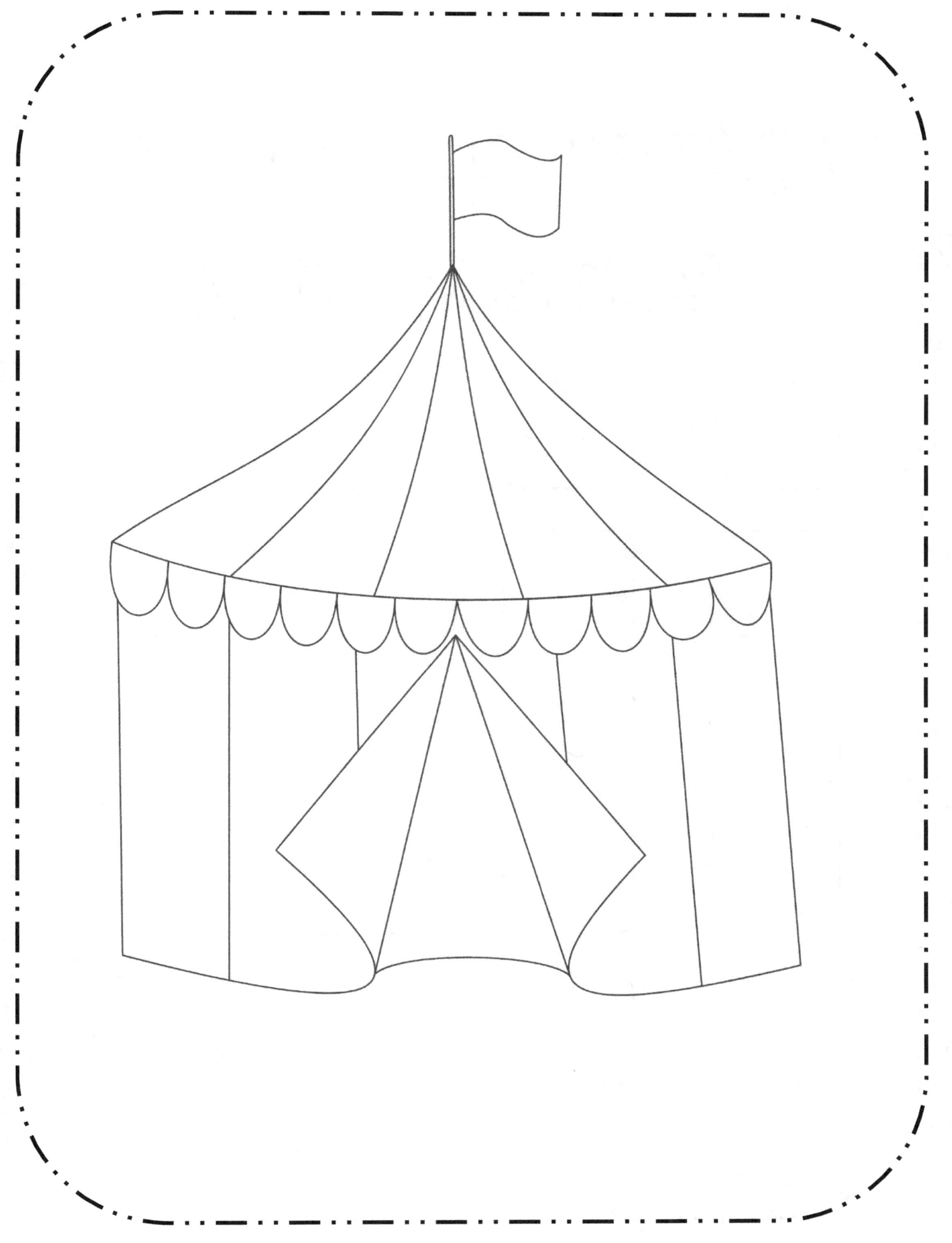

Try Your Coloring Pencil Before Coloring

Try Your Coloring Pencil Before Coloring

Try Your Coloring Pencil
Before Coloring

CIR
CUS

Try Your Coloring Pencil
Before Coloring

Try Your Coloring Pencil Before Coloring

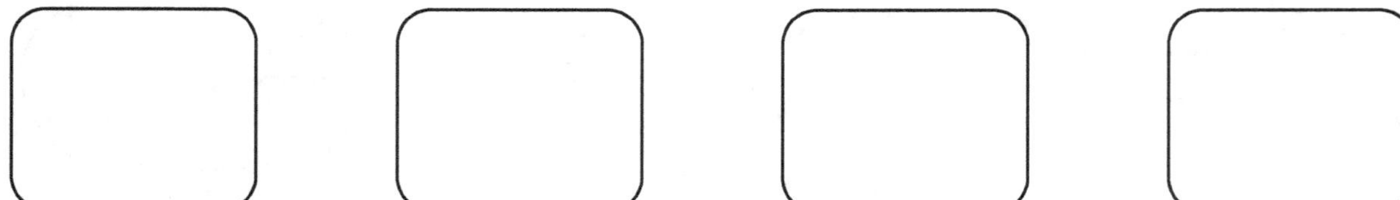

Try Your Coloring Pencil Before Coloring

Try Your Coloring Pencil Before Coloring

Try Your Coloring Pencil Before Coloring

Try Your Coloring Pencil
Before Coloring

Try Your Coloring Pencil

Before Coloring

9 798868 702728 1